Vegetarian Dinner Parties

Vegetarian Dinner Parties

SUE ASHWORTH

First published in Great Britain in 1995 by
Parragon Book Service Ltd
Unit 13-17
Avonbridge Trading Estate
Atlantic Road
Avonmouth
Bristol BS11 9QD

ISBN 1 85813 879 5

Produced by Haldane Mason, London

Printed in Italy

Acknowledgements:
Art Direction: Ron Samuels
Editor: Joanna Swinnerton
Series design: Pedro & Frances Prá-Lopez / Kingfisher Design
Page design: F14 Creative Consultants Ltd
Photography: Iain Bagwell
Styling: Rachel Jukes
Home Economist: Sue Ashworth
Assistant Home Economist: Yvonne Melville

Photographs on pp. 6, 20, 34, 48 & 62 are reproduced by permission of ZEFA Picture Library UK Ltd.

Note:
*Cup measurements in this book are for American cups. Tablespoons are assumed to be 15 ml.
Unless otherwise stated, milk is assumed to be full-fat, eggs are standard size 2 and pepper is freshly
ground black pepper.*

Contents

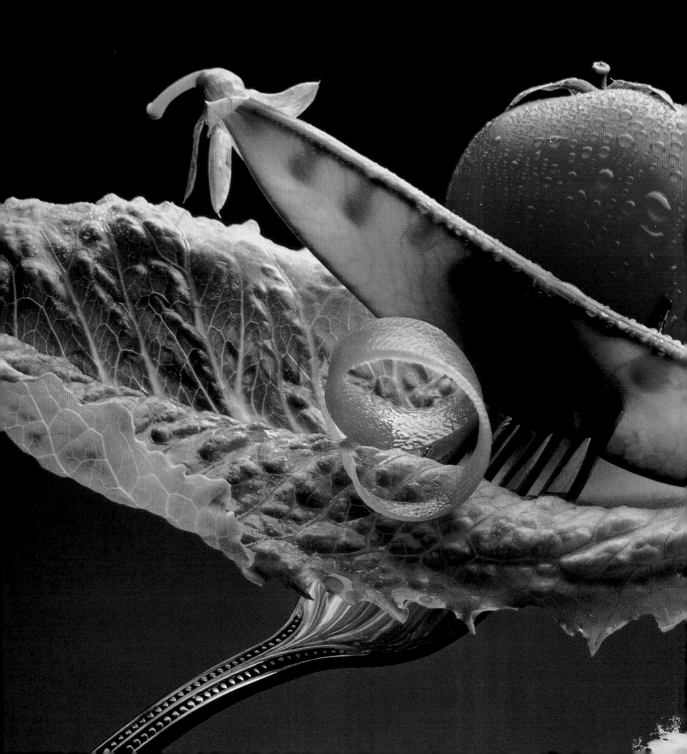

CHAPTER ONE

Dips, Nibbles & Canapés

Tempt your family or guests with a taste of things to come with these delicious ideas for vegetarian dips, nibbles and canapés – perfect for parties, buffets and for serving with pre-dinner drinks. These bite-sized nibbles make great snacks too – just the thing to have to hand when inviting a few friends around for a drink.

All the recipes are quick and simple to prepare, yet they taste really good – and they are just that little bit different from run-of-the-mill offerings. For example, the Crispy-fried Vegetables with Hot & Sweet Dipping Sauce are a delicious combination of crunchy deep-fried vegetables served with a spicy side dish. Or try Tofu & Vegetable Mini-kebabs, served with a tasty cashew nut sauce.

Presentation is very important when serving these starters. Dips can look very appetizing served in hollowed-out vegetables, such as green, red or yellow (bell) peppers and green or red cabbage. Make lots of fresh vegetable crudités for variety, crunch and colour (leftovers can always be used in soups or salads). Just before serving, garnish with fresh herbs to give them a 'fresh from the garden' look, which adds an attractive finishing flourish.

Opposite: Bite-sized food makes a tempting prelude to any meal.

STEP 1

STEP 2

STEP 3

STEP 4

FIERY SALSA WITH TORTILLA CHIPS

Make this Mexican-style salsa to perk up jaded palates. Its lively flavours really get the tastebuds going!

SERVES 6

2 small red chillies
1 tbsp lime or lemon juice
2 large ripe avocados
5 cm/2 inch piece of cucumber
2 tomatoes, peeled
1 small garlic clove, crushed
few drops of Tabasco sauce
salt and pepper
lime or lemon slices to garnish
tortilla chips to serve

1 Remove and discard the stem and seeds from 1 chilli. Chop very finely and place in a mixing bowl. To make a chilli 'flower' for garnish, slice the remaining chilli from the stem to the tip several times without removing the stem. Place in a bowl of cold water, so that the 'petals' open out.

2 Add the lime or lemon juice to the mixing bowl. Halve, stone (pit) and peel the avocados. Add to the mixing bowl and mash with a fork. (The lime or lemon juice prevents the avocado from turning brown.)

3 Chop the cucumber and tomatoes finely and add to the avocado mixture with the crushed garlic.

4 Season the dip to taste with Tabasco sauce, salt and pepper.

5 Transfer the dip to a serving bowl. Garnish with slices of lime or lemon and the chilli flower. Put the bowl on a large plate, surround with tortilla chips and serve.

CHILLIES

If you're not keen on hot, spicy flavours, make a milder version by omitting the chillies and Tabasco sauce. Take care when handling fresh chillies, as they can irritate the skin. Prepare them quickly and wash your hands afterwards. Be careful to avoid touching your eyes during preparation.

STEP 1

STEP 2

STEP 3

STEP 4

BAKED AUBERGINE (EGGPLANT), BASIL & MOZZARELLA ROLLS

Thin slices of aubergine (eggplant) are fried in olive oil and garlic, and then topped with pesto sauce and finely sliced Mozzarella cheese.

SERVES 4

2 aubergines (eggplant), sliced thinly
   lengthways
5 tbsp olive oil
1 garlic clove, crushed
4 tbsp pesto sauce
175 g/6 oz/1½ cups Mozzarella cheese,
   grated
a few basil leaves, torn into pieces
salt and pepper
fresh basil leaves to garnish

1 Spread out the slices of aubergine (eggplant) on a work surface (counter). Sprinkle liberally with salt and leave for 10–15 minutes to extract the bitter juices. Turn the slices over and repeat. Rinse well with cold water and drain on paper towels.

2 Heat the olive oil in a large frying pan (skillet) and add the garlic. Fry the aubergine (eggplant) slices lightly on both sides, a few at a time. Drain them on paper towels.

3 Spread the pesto sauce on to one side of the aubergine (eggplant) slices. Top with the grated Mozzarella cheese and sprinkle with the torn basil leaves. Season with a little salt and

pepper. Roll up the slices and secure with wooden cocktail sticks (toothpicks).

4 Arrange the aubergine (eggplant) rolls in a greased ovenproof baking dish. Place in a preheated oven at 180°C/350°F/Gas Mark 4 and bake for 8–10 minutes.

5 Transfer the rolls to a warmed serving plate. Scatter with fresh basil leaves and serve at once.

GRATED CHEESE

If you wish, buy ready-grated cheese from your supermarket or delicatessen, as it can be quite tricky to grate it yourself. Otherwise, you may find it easier to slice the Mozzarella thinly.

STEP 1

STEP 2

STEP 3

STEP 4

CRISPY-FRIED VEGETABLES WITH HOT & SWEET DIPPING SAUCE

A Thai-style dipping sauce makes the perfect accompaniment to fresh vegetables in season coated in a light batter and deep-fried.

SERVES 4

vegetable oil, for deep-frying
500 g / 1 lb selection of vegetables, such as cauliflower, broccoli, mushrooms, courgettes (zucchini), (bell) peppers and baby corn, cut into even-sized pieces

BATTER:
125 g / 4 oz / 1 cup plain (all-purpose) flour
¹/₂ tsp salt
1 tsp caster (superfine) sugar
1 tsp baking powder
3 tbsp vegetable oil
200 ml / 7 fl oz / scant 1 cup warm water

SAUCE:
6 tbsp light malt vinegar
2 tbsp Thai fish sauce or light soy sauce
2 tbsp water
1 tbsp soft brown sugar
pinch of salt
2 garlic cloves, crushed
2 tsp grated fresh root ginger
2 red chillies, deseeded and chopped finely
2 tbsp chopped fresh coriander (cilantro)

1 To make the batter, sift the flour, salt, sugar and baking powder into a large bowl. Add the oil and most of the water. Whisk together to make a smooth batter, adding extra water to give it the consistency of single cream. Chill for 20–30 minutes.

2 Meanwhile, make the sauce. Heat the vinegar, fish sauce or soy sauce, water, sugar and salt until boiling. Remove from the heat and leave to cool.

3 Mix together the garlic, ginger, chillies and coriander (cilantro) in a small serving bowl. Add the cooled vinegar mixture and stir together.

4 Heat the vegetable oil for deep-frying in a wok or deep-fat fryer. Dip the prepared vegetables in the batter and fry them, a few at a time, until crisp and golden – about 2 minutes. Drain on paper towels.

5 Serve the vegetables accompanied by the dipping sauce.

CORIANDER (CILANTRO)

Fresh coriander (cilantro) is a wonderful herb, with a pungent, distinctive flavour. You can use the stem and root as well as the leaves – just make sure that they are thoroughly cleaned before use.

MINT & CANNELLINI BEAN DIP

This dip is ideal for pre-dinner drinks or for handing around at a party, accompanied by crisps and colourful vegetable crudités. For speed and convenience you could use canned beans if preferred, but remember to double the quantity.

STEP 2

SERVES 6

175 g/6 oz dried cannellini beans
1 small garlic clove, crushed
1 bunch spring onions (scallions), chopped
  roughly
a handful of fresh mint leaves
2 tbsp tahini (sesame seed paste)
2 tbsp olive oil
1 tsp ground cumin
1 tsp ground coriander
lemon juice
salt and pepper
sprigs of fresh mint to garnish
fresh vegetable crudités, such as cauliflower
  florets, carrots, cucumber, radishes and
  (bell) peppers

1 Soak the cannellini beans overnight in plenty of cold water.

2 Rinse and drain the beans, put them into a large saucepan and cover them with cold water. Bring to the boil and boil rapidly for 10 minutes. Reduce the heat, cover and simmer for 1½–2 hours until tender.

3 Drain the beans and transfer them to a bowl or food processor. Add the garlic, spring onions (scallions), mint, tahini and olive oil.

4 Blend the mixture for about 15 seconds, or mash well by hand, until smooth.

5 Transfer the mixture to a bowl and season with ground cumin, ground coriander, lemon juice, salt and pepper, according to taste. Mix well, cover and leave in a cool place for 30 minutes to allow the flavours to develop.

6 Spoon the dip into serving bowls, garnish with sprigs of fresh mint and surround with the vegetable crudités.

CANNED BEANS

If using canned cannellini beans, use 2 × 425g/14 oz cans. Drain and rinse well. Add to the bowl or food processor at step 3. Chick-peas (garbanzo beans) may be used as an alternative.

STEP 3

STEP 4

STEP 5

STEP 1

STEP 2

STEP 4

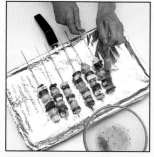

STEP 5

TOFU & VEGETABLE MINI-KEBABS

Cubes of smoked tofu are speared on bamboo satay sticks with crisp vegetables, basted with lemon juice and olive oil, and then grilled. The cashew nut sauce can be drizzled over the kebabs or used as a dip.

SERVES 6

300 g / 10 oz smoked tofu, cut into cubes
1 large red and 1 large yellow (bell) pepper, deseeded and cut into small squares
175 g / 6 oz button mushrooms, wiped
1 small courgette (zucchini), sliced
finely grated rind and juice of 1 lemon
3 tbsp olive oil
1 tbsp chopped parsley
1 tsp caster (superfine) sugar
salt and pepper
sprigs of parsley to garnish

SAUCE:
125 g / 4 oz / 1 cup cashew nuts
15 g / ¹/₂ oz / 1 tbsp butter
1 garlic clove, crushed
1 shallot, chopped finely
1 tsp ground coriander
1 tsp ground cumin
1 tbsp caster (superfine) sugar
1 tbsp desiccated (shredded) coconut
150 ml / ¹/₄ pint / ²/₃ cup natural yogurt

1 Thread the tofu cubes, (bell) peppers, mushrooms and courgettes (zucchini) on to bamboo satay sticks. Arrange them in a shallow dish.

2 Mix together the lemon rind and juice, oil, parsley and sugar. Season well with salt and pepper. Pour over the kebabs, and brush them with the mixture. Leave for 10 minutes.

3 To make the sauce, scatter the cashew nuts on to a baking sheet and toast them until lightly browned.

4 Melt the butter in a saucepan and cook the garlic and shallot gently until softened. Transfer to a blender or food processor and add the nuts, coriander, cumin, sugar, coconut and yogurt. Blend until combined, about 15 seconds. Alternatively, chop the nuts finely and mix with the remaining ingredients.

5 Place the tofu kebabs under a preheated grill (broiler) and cook, turning and basting with the lemon juice mixture, until lightly browned. Garnish with sprigs of parsley, and serve with the cashew nut sauce.

TIME SAVER

If you have a lot to do, it can help to make the sauce and prepare the kebabs in advance – then you can cook them in just a few minutes when they are needed.

STEP 1

STEP 2

STEP 3

STEP 4

HERB, TOASTED NUT & PAPRIKA CHEESE NIBBLES

These tiny cheese balls are rolled in fresh herbs, toasted nuts or paprika to make tasty nibbles for parties, buffets, or pre-dinner drinks.

SERVES 4

125 g/4 oz Ricotta cheese
125 g/4 oz Double Gloucester (brick)
  cheese, grated finely
2 tsp chopped parsley
60 g/2 oz/¹/₂ cup chopped mixed nuts
3 tbsp chopped fresh herbs, such as parsley,
  chives, marjoram, lovage and chervil
2 tbsp mild paprika
pepper
sprigs of fresh herbs to garnish

1 Mix together the Ricotta and Double Gloucester (brick) cheeses. Add the parsley and pepper, and work together until combined.

2 Form the mixture into small balls. Cover and chill for about 20 minutes to firm.

3 Scatter the chopped nuts on to a baking sheet and place them under a preheated grill (broiler) until lightly browned. Take care as they can easily burn. Leave them to cool.

4 Sprinkle the nuts, herbs and paprika into 3 separate small bowls. Divide the cheese balls into 3 equal piles and then roll 1 quantity in

the nuts, 1 quantity in the herbs and 1 quantity in the paprika.

5 Arrange on a serving platter. Chill until ready to serve, and then garnish with sprigs of fresh herbs.

CHEESE AND NUTS

You can buy small bags of chopped mixed nuts at most supermarkets. Alternatively, buy whole, blanched nuts and chop them finely in a food processor or blender.

To ring the changes, use soft cheese instead of Ricotta, and mature Cheddar or Red Leicester instead of the Double Gloucester (brick) cheese.

CHAPTER TWO

Starters & Soups

With so many fresh ingredients readily available, it is very easy to create some deliciously different starters and soups to make the perfect introduction to a vegetarian meal. The ideas in this chapter are an inspiration to cook and a treat to eat, and they give an edge to the appetite that makes the main course even more enjoyable.

When choosing a starter, make sure that you provide a good balance of flavours, colours and textures that offer variety and contrast. Decide whether you want to serve a hot or a cold starter – generally it is a good idea to begin with a hot course if the main one is cold, and vice versa. Balance the nature of the recipes too – a rich main course would be best if preceded by a light starter, just sufficient to interest the palate and stimulate the tastebuds.

Give some consideration to the amount of food you are likely to serve: you could easily overwhelm appetites by serving portions that are too large, especially if you plan to make a dessert too. The recipes in this section will give an impressive start to a special meal, especially if you can spend a little extra time arranging and garnishing the food attractively. Then these delicious recipes will look as good as they taste.

Opposite: *Choose from a wide range of fresh ingredients, and your cooking will be rich in both colour and flavour.*

STEP 1

STEP 2

STEP 3

STEP 5

PLUM TOMATO SOUP

Homemade tomato soup is easy to make and always tastes better than bought varieties. Try this version with its Mediterranean influences – plum tomatoes, red onions and fresh Italian herbs. Serve it with warm ciabatta bread topped with olive and hazelnut spread.

SERVES 4

2 tbsp olive oil
2 red onions, chopped
2 celery sticks, chopped
1 carrot, chopped
500 g/ 1 lb fresh plum tomatoes, halved
750 ml / 1¼ pints/ 3 cups vegetable stock
1 tbsp chopped fresh oregano, or 1 tsp dried oregano
1 tbsp chopped fresh basil, or 1 tsp dried basil
150 ml/ ¼ pint/ ⅔ cup dry white wine
2 tsp caster (superfine) sugar
125 g/ 4 oz/ 1 cup hazelnuts, toasted
125 g/ 4 oz/ 1 cup black or green olives
handful of fresh basil leaves
1 tbsp olive oil
1 loaf ciabatta bread (Italian-style loaf)
salt and pepper
sprigs of fresh basil to garnish

1 Heat the olive oil in a large saucepan and fry the chopped onions, celery and carrot gently until softened.

2 Add the tomatoes, stock, chopped herbs, wine and sugar. Bring to the boil, then cover and simmer gently for about 20 minutes.

3 Place the toasted hazelnuts in a blender or food processor with the olives and basil leaves and process until combined, but not too smooth. Alternatively, chop the nuts, olives and basil leaves finely and pound in a mortar and pestle, then turn into a small bowl. Add the olive oil, process for a few seconds or beat thoroughly, and then turn the mixture into a serving bowl.

4 Warm the ciabatta bread in a preheated oven at 190°C/375°F/ Gas Mark 5 for 3–4 minutes.

5 Blend the soup in a blender or a food processor, or press through a sieve, until smooth. Check the seasoning, adding salt and pepper according to taste. Ladle into 4 warmed soup bowls. Garnish with sprigs of basil. Slice the warm bread and spread with the olive and hazelnut paste. Serve with the soup.

TOMATOES

If you wish, remove the skins from the tomatoes with a fork while they are still in the pan. If you cannot buy fresh plum tomatoes, use ordinary tomatoes or a 425g/14 oz can of plum tomatoes instead.

STEP 1

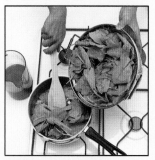

STEP 2

STEP 4

STEP 5

SPINACH & MASCARPONE SOUP

Spinach is the basis for this delicious soup, which has creamy Mascarpone cheese stirred through it to give it the most wonderful texture and flavour. Try sorrel or watercress instead of spinach for a pleasant change.

Serves 4

60 g / 2 oz / $\frac{1}{4}$ cup butter
1 bunch spring onions (scallions), trimmed
  and chopped
2 celery sticks, chopped
350 g / 12 oz / 3 cups spinach or sorrel, or
  3 bunches watercress
900 ml / 1$\frac{1}{2}$ pints / 3$\frac{1}{2}$ cups vegetable stock
250 g / 8 oz / 1 cup Mascarpone cheese
1 tbsp olive oil
2 slices thick-cut bread, cut into cubes
$\frac{1}{2}$ tsp caraway seeds
salt and pepper
sesame bread sticks to serve

1 Melt half the butter in a very large saucepan. Add the spring onions (scallions) and celery, and cook gently for about 5 minutes, until softened.

2 Pack the spinach, sorrel or watercress into the saucepan. Add the stock and bring to the boil; then reduce the heat and simmer, covered, for 15–20 minutes.

3 Transfer the soup to a blender or food processor and blend until smooth, or rub through a sieve. Return to the saucepan.

4 Add the Mascarpone cheese to the soup and heat gently, stirring, until smooth and blended. Taste and season with salt and pepper.

5 Heat the remaining butter with the oil in a frying pan. Add the bread cubes and fry in the hot fat until golden brown, adding the caraway seeds towards the end of cooking, so that they do not burn.

6 Ladle the soup into 4 warmed bowls. Sprinkle with the croûtons and serve at once, accompanied by the sesame bread sticks.

VARIATIONS

Any leafy vegetable can be used to make this soup to give variations to the flavour. For anyone who grows their own vegetables, it is the perfect recipe for experimenting with a glut of produce. Try young beetroot (beet) leaves or surplus lettuces for a change.

CHEESE, GARLIC & HERB PATE

This wonderful soft cheese pâté is fragrant with the aroma of fresh herbs and garlic. Pile it on to small plates, garnish with salad and serve with crisp triangles of Melba toast to make the perfect starter.

STEP 1

SERVES 4

15 g/¹/₂ oz butter
1 garlic clove, crushed
3 spring onions (scallions), chopped finely
2 tbsp chopped mixed fresh herbs, such as parsley, chives, marjoram, oregano and basil
125 g/4 oz/¹/₂ cup cream cheese
175 g/6 oz/1¹/₂ cups mature Cheddar cheese, grated finely
pepper
4–6 slices of white bread from a medium-cut sliced loaf
mixed salad leaves and cherry tomatoes, to serve

TO GARNISH:
ground paprika
sprigs of fresh herbs

1 Melt the butter in a small frying pan (skillet) and fry the garlic and spring onions (scallions) together gently for 3–4 minutes, until softened. Allow to cool.

2 Put the cream cheese into a large mixing bowl and beat until soft. Then add the garlic and spring onions (scallions). Stir in the herbs, mixing well.

3 Add the Cheddar cheese and work the mixture together to form a stiff paste. Cover and chill until ready to serve.

4 To make the Melba toast, toast the slices of bread on both sides, and then cut off the crusts. Using a sharp bread knife, cut through the slices horizontally to make very thin slices. Cut into triangles and then grill (broil) the untoasted sides lightly.

5 Arrange the mixed salad leaves on 4 serving plates with the cherry tomatoes. Pile the cheese pâté on top and sprinkle with a little paprika. Garnish with sprigs of fresh herbs and serve with the Melba toast.

STEP 2

STEP 3

CHEESE

You can vary this recipe by choosing different cheeses – try Italian Ricotta in place of the cream cheese or substitute Double Gloucester (brick) or Red Leicester cheese for the Cheddar. Do make sure that the hard cheese is very finely grated for best results.

STEP 4

STEP 2

STEP 3

STEP 5

STEP 6

LEEK & SUN-DRIED TOMATO TIMBALES

Angel-hair pasta, known as cappellini, is mixed with fried leeks, sun-dried tomatoes, fresh oregano and beaten eggs, and baked in ramekins.

SERVES 4

90 g/ 3 oz angel-hair pasta (cappellini)
30 g/ 1 oz/ 2 tbsp butter
1 tbsp olive oil
1 large leek, sliced finely
60 g/ 2 oz/¹/₂ cup sun-dried tomatoes in oil, drained and chopped
1 tbsp chopped fresh oregano or 1 tsp dried oregano
2 eggs, beaten
90 ml/ 3¹/₂ fl oz/ generous ¹/₃ cup single (light) cream
1 tbsp grated Parmesan cheese
lettuce leaves to serve
salt and pepper

SAUCE:
1 small onion, chopped finely
1 small garlic clove, crushed
350 g/ 12 oz tomatoes, peeled and chopped
1 tsp mixed dried Italian herbs
4 tbsp dry white wine

1 Cook the pasta in plenty of boiling, lightly salted water for about 3 minutes until *al dente* (just tender). Drain and rinse with cold water to cool quickly.

2 Meanwhile, heat the butter and oil in a frying pan (skillet). Fry the leek gently until softened and cooked, about 5–6 minutes. Add the sun-dried tomatoes and oregano, and cook for a further 2 minutes. Remove from the heat.

3 Add the leek mixture to the pasta. Stir in the beaten eggs, cream and Parmesan cheese. Season with salt and pepper. Divide between 4 greased ramekin dishes or dariole moulds.

4 Place the dishes in a roasting tin with enough warm water to come halfway up their sides. Bake in a preheated oven at 180°C/350°F/Gas Mark 4 for about 30 minutes, until set.

5 To make the tomato sauce, fry the onion and garlic in the remaining butter and oil until softened. Add the tomatoes, herbs and wine. Cover and cook gently for about 20 minutes until pulpy. Blend in a food processor until smooth, or press through a sieve.

6 Turn out the timbales on to 4 warmed serving plates. Pour over a little sauce and garnish with sprigs of oregano. Serve with the lettuce leaves.

STEP 1

STEP 2

STEP 3

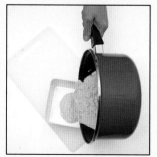

STEP 4

AVOCADO CREAM TERRINE

*The smooth, rich taste of ripe avocados combines well with thick,
creamy yogurt and single (light) cream to make this impressive terrine.*

SERVES 6

4 tbsp cold water
2 tsp gelozone (vegetarian gelatine)
1 tbsp lemon juice
4 tbsp mayonnaise
150 ml /¹/₄ pint/²/₃ cup thick creamy
    natural yogurt
150 ml /¹/₄ pint/²/₃ cup single (light) cream
2 ripe avocados
salt and pepper
mixed salad leaves (greens) to serve

TO GARNISH:
cucumber slices
nasturtium flowers

1 Assemble the water, gelozone,
lemon juice, mayonnaise, yogurt
and cream. Peel the avocados and
remove the stones (pits). Place all these
ingredients in a blender or food
processor, or a large bowl.

2 Process for about 10–15 seconds,
or beat by hand, until smooth.

3 Transfer the mixture to a small
saucepan and heat gently, stirring
constantly, until just boiling.

4 Pour the mixture into a 900 ml/
1¹/₂ pint/3¹/₂ cup plastic food
storage box or terrine. Allow to cool and
set, and then refrigerate until chilled –
about 1¹/₂–2 hours.

5 Turn the mixture out of its
container and cut into neat slices.
Arrange a bed of salad leaves (greens) on
6 serving plates. Place a slice of avocado
terrine on top and garnish with
cucumber slices and nasturtium flowers.

AVOCADOS

Avocados soon turn brown, so it is
important to mix them with the lemon
juice as soon as they are peeled and
mashed to prevent this from happening.

STEP 1

STEP 2

STEP 3

STEP 5

BUTTER-CRUST TARTLETS WITH FETA CHEESE

These crispy-baked bread cases, filled with sliced tomatoes, Feta cheese, black olives and quail's eggs, are quick to make and taste delicious.

SERVES 4

8 slices of bread from a medium-cut large loaf
125 g/4 oz/¹/₂ cup butter, melted
125 g/4 oz Feta cheese, cut into small cubes
4 cherry tomatoes, cut into wedges
8 stoned (pitted) black or green olives, halved
8 quail's eggs, hard-boiled
2 tbsp olive oil
1 tbsp wine vinegar
1 tsp wholegrain mustard
pinch of caster (superfine) sugar
salt and pepper
sprigs of parsley to garnish

1 Remove the crusts from the slices of bread. Trim the bread into squares and flatten each piece with a rolling pin.

2 Brush the pieces of bread with melted butter, and then arrange them in bun or muffin tins. Press a piece of crumpled foil into each bread case to secure in place. Bake in a preheated oven at 190°C/375°F/Gas Mark 5 for about 10 minutes, or until crisp and browned.

3 Meanwhile, mix together the Feta cheese, tomatoes and olives. Shell the eggs and quarter them. Mix together the olive oil, vinegar, mustard and sugar. Season with salt and pepper.

4 Remove the bread cases from the oven and discard the foil. Leave to cool.

5 Just before serving, fill the cooked bread cases with the cheese and tomato mixture. Arrange the eggs on top and spoon over the dressing. Garnish with sprigs of parsley.

BITE-SIZE

For canapés and nibbles, the bread can be cut into smaller pieces and used to line mini muffin tins. They can then be filled with mixtures of your choice. (Try using the Cheese, Garlic & Herb Pâté on page 27.)

CHAPTER THREE

Main Courses

Anyone who ever thought that vegetarian meals were dull will be proved wrong by the rich variety of dishes in this chapter. In these recipes, you will recognize influences from Indian, Italian, Greek and Indonesian cooking and although you may not have used some of the ingredients often, you should have no difficulty in buying them locally. With luck you will discover a whole range of new ingredients that can easily be added to your shopping-list and used to great effect in any number of dishes, both new and old. The Indonesian Chestnut & Vegetable Stir-fry, for example, may introduce you to sesame oil for the first time. It is fragrant and flavoursome and adds a new dimension of subtlety that, once tried, you will want to use all the time in your stir-fries.

While each recipe may encourage you to try new ingredients, don't be afraid to substitute some of your own favourites where appropriate. For instance, you may prefer to make the Almond & Sesame Nut Roast with peanuts instead of almonds, for a more economical everyday occasion. There is no reason why you can't experiment and enjoy adding your own signature to these imaginative ideas.

Opposite: *Select the freshest basic ingredients that you can find to be sure of an unforgettable dinner party dish.*

STEP 1

STEP 2

STEP 3

STEP 4

TAGLIATELLE TRICOLORE WITH BROCCOLI & BLUE CHEESE SAUCE

Some of the simplest and most satisfying dishes are made with pasta. This delicious combination of tagliatelle with its Gorgonzola and Mascarpone cheese sauce is one of them.

SERVES 4

300 g/10 oz tagliatelle tricolore (plain, spinach- and tomato-flavoured noodles)
250 g/8 oz broccoli, broken into small florets
350g/12 oz/1½ cups Mascarpone cheese
125 g/4 oz/1 cup Gorgonzola cheese, chopped
1 tbsp chopped fresh oregano
30 g/1 oz/2 tbsp butter
sprigs of fresh oregano to garnish
grated Parmesan cheese to serve
salt and pepper

1 Cook the tagliatelle in plenty of boiling, lightly salted water until just tender, according to the instructions on the packet. The Italians call this *al dente*, which literally means 'to the tooth'.

2 Meanwhile, cook the broccoli florets in a small amount of lightly salted, boiling water. Avoid overcooking the broccoli, so that it retains its colour and texture.

3 Heat the Mascarpone and Gorgonzola cheeses together gently in a large saucepan until they are melted.

Stir in the oregano and season with salt and pepper.

4 Drain the pasta thoroughly. Return it to the saucepan and add the butter, tossing the tagliatelle to coat it. Drain the broccoli well and add to the pasta with the sauce, tossing gently to mix.

5 Divide the pasta between 4 warmed serving plates. Garnish with sprigs of fresh oregano and serve with Parmesan cheese.

A L T E R N A T I V E S

Choose your favourite pasta shapes to use in this recipe as an alternative to tagliatelle. If you prefer, substitute a creamy blue Stilton for the Gorgonzola.

36

STEP 1

STEP 2

STEP 3

STEP 4

MUSHROOM & PINE KERNEL TARTS

These mushroom-filled filo pastry tarts make a delicious main course meal. Different varieties of mushroom are becoming more widely available in supermarkets, so use this recipe to make the most of them.

SERVES 4

500 g/1 lb frozen filo pastry, thawed
125 g/4 oz/½ cup butter, melted
1 tbsp hazelnut oil
30 g/1 oz pine kernels
350 g/12 oz mixed mushrooms, such as
   buttons, chestnut, oyster and shiitake
2 tsp chopped fresh parsley
250 g/8 oz soft goat's cheese
salt and pepper
sprigs of parsley to garnish
lettuce, tomatoes, cucumber and spring
   onions (scallions) to serve

1 Cut the sheets of filo pastry into pieces about 10 cm/4 inches square and use them to line 4 individual tart tins, brushing each layer of pastry with melted butter. Line the tins with foil or baking parchment and baking beans. Bake in a preheated oven at 200°C/400°F/Gas Mark 6 for about 6–8 minutes, or until light golden brown. Remove the tarts from the oven and take out the foil or parchment and beans carefully. Reduce the oven temperature to 180°C/350°F/Gas Mark 4.

2 Put any remaining butter into a large saucepan with the hazelnut oil and fry the pine kernels (nuts) gently until golden brown. Lift them out with a perforated spoon and drain them on paper towels.

3 Add the mushrooms to the saucepan and cook them gently, stirring frequently, for about 4–5 minutes. Add the chopped parsley and season to taste with salt and pepper.

4 Spoon an equal amount of goat's cheese into the base of each cooked filo tart. Divide the mushrooms between them and scatter the pine kernels over the top.

5 Return the tarts to the oven for 5 minutes to heat through, and then serve them, garnished with sprigs of parsley. Serve with lettuce, tomatoes, cucumber and spring onions (scallions).

FILO PASTRY

Filo pastry is easy to use, but handle it carefully as it is quite delicate. As you use the pastry, keep it covered with clingfilm (plastic wrap) or a damp cloth to prevent it from drying out.

STEP 1

STEP 2

STEP 3

STEP 4

RICOTTA & SPINACH PARCELS

Ricotta cheese and spinach make a great flavour combination, especially when encased in light puff-pastry parcels. Gently fried onions and green peppercorns add to the success of this dish.

SERVES 4

350 g/12 oz/3 cups spinach, trimmed and washed thoroughly
30 g/1 oz/2 tbsp butter
1 small onion, chopped finely
1 tsp green peppercorns
500 g/1 lb puff pastry
250 g/8 oz/1 cup Ricotta cheese
1 egg, beaten
salt
sprigs of fresh herbs to garnish
fresh vegetables to serve

1 Pack the spinach into a large saucepan. Add a little salt and a very small amount of water and cook until wilted. Drain well, cool and then squeeze out any excess moisture with the back of a spoon. Chop roughly.

2 Melt the butter in a small saucepan and fry the onion gently until softened, but not browned. Add the green peppercorns and cook for 2 more minutes. Remove from the heat, add the spinach and mix together.

3 Roll out the puff pastry thinly on a lightly floured work surface and cut into 4 squares, each 18 cm/7 inches across. Place a quarter of the spinach mixture in the centre of each square and top with a quarter of the cheese.

4 Brush a little beaten egg around the edges of the pastry squares and bring the corners together to form parcels. Press the edges together firmly to seal. Lift the parcels on to a greased baking sheet, brush with beaten egg and bake in a preheated oven at 200°C/400°F/Gas Mark 6 for 20–25 minutes, until risen and golden brown.

5 Serve hot, garnished with sprigs of fresh herbs and accompanied by fresh vegetables.

DECORATION

Any pastry trimmings can be rolled out and cut into leaves to garnish the parcels. Brush with beaten egg to glaze them.

Fresh green peppercorns can be bought in small jars, preserved in brine. They have a milder flavour than black peppercorns and are ideal when used whole or lightly crushed in a variety of savoury recipes.

INDIAN CURRY FEAST

This vegetable curry is quick and easy to prepare, and it tastes superb. If you make a colourful Indian salad to accompany it and a cool mint raita to refresh the palate, you have the makings of a real feast!

STEP 1

SERVES 4

1 tbsp vegetable oil
2 garlic cloves, crushed
1 onion, chopped
3 celery sticks, sliced
1 apple, chopped
1 tbsp medium-strength curry powder
1 tsp ground ginger
125 g/4 oz dwarf (thin) green beans, sliced
250 g/8 oz cauliflower, broken into florets
250 g/8 oz potatoes, cut into cubes
175 g/6 oz/2 cups mushrooms, wiped and
    sliced
400 g/13 oz can chick-peas (garbanzo
    beans), drained
600 ml/1 pint/2½ cups vegetable stock
1 tbsp tomato purée (paste)
30 g/1 oz sultanas (golden raisins)
175 g/6 oz basmati rice
1 tbsp garam masala

SALAD:
4 tomatoes, chopped
1 green chilli, deseeded and finely chopped
7 cm/3 inch piece of cucumber, chopped
1 tbsp fresh coriander (cilantro)
4 spring onions (scallions), trimmed and
    chopped

MINT RAITA:
150 ml/¼ pint/⅔ cup natural yogurt

STEP 2

1 tbsp chopped fresh mint
sprigs of fresh mint to garnish

1 Heat the oil in a large saucepan and fry the garlic, onion, celery and apple gently for 3–4 minutes. Add the curry powder and ginger, and cook gently for 1 more minute.

2 Add the remaining ingredients except the rice and garam masala. Bring to the boil, then reduce the heat. Cover and simmer for 35–40 minutes.

3 To make the salad, combine all the ingredients. Cover and chill.

4 To make the raita, mix the yogurt and mint together. Transfer to a serving dish, then cover and chill.

5 Cook the rice in boiling, lightly salted water until just tender, according to the instructions on the packet. Drain thoroughly.

6 Just before serving, stir the garam masala into the curry. Divide between 4 warmed serving plates, and serve with the salad, mint raita and rice. Garnish the raita with fresh mint.

STEP 4

STEP 6

STEP 1

STEP 2

STEP 3

STEP 4

ALMOND & SESAME NUT ROAST

Toasted almonds are combined with sesame seeds, rice and vegetables in this tasty vegetarian roast. Serve it with a delicious onion and mushroom sauce to reap the compliments.

SERVES 4

2 tbsp sesame or olive oil
1 small onion, chopped finely
60 g/2 oz/scant ¼ cup risotto rice
300 ml/½ pint/1¼ cups vegetable stock
1 large carrot, grated
1 large leek, trimmed and chopped finely
2 tsp sesame seeds, toasted
90 g/3 oz/¾ cup chopped almonds, toasted
60 g/2 oz/½ cup ground almonds
90 g/3 oz/¾ cup mature (sharp) Cheddar
   cheese, grated
2 eggs, beaten
1 tsp dried mixed herbs
salt and pepper
sprigs of flat-leaf (Italian) parsley to garnish
fresh vegetables to serve

SAUCE:
30 g/1 oz/2 tbsp butter
1 small onion, chopped finely
125 g/4 oz/1¼ cup mushrooms, chopped
   finely
30 g/1 oz/¼ cup plain (all-purpose) flour
300 ml/½ pint/1¼ cups vegetable stock

1 Heat the oil in a large frying pan (skillet) and fry the onion gently for 2–3 minutes. Add the rice and cook gently for 5–6 minutes, stirring frequently.

2 Add the vegetable stock, bring to the boil and then simmer for about 15 minutes, or until the rice is tender. Add a little extra water if necessary. Remove from the heat and transfer to a large mixing bowl.

3 Add the carrot, leek, sesame seeds, almonds, cheese, beaten eggs and herbs to the mixture. Mix well and season with salt and pepper. Transfer the mixture to a greased 500 g/1 lb loaf tin, levelling the surface. Bake in a preheated oven at 180°C/350°F/Gas Mark 4 for about 1 hour, until set and firm. Leave in the tin for 10 minutes.

4 To make the sauce, melt the butter in a small saucepan and fry the onion until dark golden brown. Add the mushrooms and cook for a further 2 minutes. Stir in the flour, cook gently for 1 minute and then gradually add the stock. Bring to the boil, stirring constantly, until thickened and blended. Season to taste.

5 Turn out the nut roast, slice and serve on warmed plates with fresh vegetables, accompanied by the sauce. Garnish with sprigs of flat-leaf (Italian) parsley.

STEP 1

STEP 2

STEP 3

STEP 4

INDONESIAN CHESTNUT & VEGETABLE STIR-FRY WITH PEANUT SAUCE

This colourful, spicy stir-fry has an Indonesian influence, with the shallots, chillies, ginger, fresh coriander (cilantro) and limes.

SERVES 4

SAUCE:
125 g/4 oz/1 cup unsalted peanuts, roasted
    and ground
2 tsp hot chilli sauce
180 ml/6 fl oz/³/₄ cup coconut milk
2 tbsp soy sauce
1 tbsp ground coriander
pinch of ground turmeric
1 tbsp dark muscovado sugar

STIR-FRY:
3 tbsp sesame oil
3–4 shallots, finely sliced
1 garlic clove, finely sliced
1–2 red chillies, deseeded and finely chopped
1 large carrot, cut into fine strips
1 yellow & 1 red (bell) pepper, deseeded and
    cut into fine strips
1 courgette (zucchini), cut into fine strips
125 g/4 oz sugar snap peas, trimmed
7.5 cm/3 inch piece of cucumber, cut into
    strips
250 g/8 oz oyster mushrooms, wiped and
    torn into small pieces, if large
250 g/8 oz canned whole peeled chestnuts,
    drained
2 tsp grated fresh root ginger
finely grated rind and juice of 1 lime
1 tbsp chopped fresh coriander (cilantro)

salt and pepper
slices of lime, to garnish

1 To make the sauce, put all the ingredients into a small pan. Heat gently and simmer for 3–4 minutes.

2 Heat the sesame oil in a wok or large frying pan (skillet). Add the shallots, garlic and chillies and stir-fry for 2 minutes.

3 Add the carrot, (bell) peppers, courgette (zucchini) and sugar snap peas to the wok or pan (skillet) and stir-fry for 2 more minutes.

4 Add all the remaining ingredients to the wok or pan (skillet) and stir-fry briskly for about 5 minutes, or until the vegetables are crisp, yet crunchy.

5 Divide the stir-fry between 4 warmed serving plates, and garnish with slices of lime. Serve with the peanut sauce.

CHAPTER FOUR

Vegetable Accompaniments

If you are running short of ideas for interesting ways to serve vegetables with your meals, these recipes will be a welcome inspiration. There is now such an abundance of fresh vegetables available all year round that there is no excuse not to serve interesting accompaniments. It is true that some produce may seem too expensive if out of season or imported from abroad, but you can always cook locally grown vegetables in unusual ways to give them a totally new treatment, and buy unusual varieties on special occasions or in small quantities. When added to other vegetables, they can make the entire dish seem more exotic.

Herbs and spices can be used to great effect with vegetables. For instance, the Stir-fried Winter Vegetables recipe is composed of familiar types of vegetable, brought to life with fresh coriander (cilantro), a deliciously fragrant herb that is becoming more easily obtainable.

These recipes need not be mere accompaniments; some are delicious enough to serve as main courses in their own right. However you choose to serve them, you won't be disappointed.

Opposite: *The range of vegetables that is now available means endless possibilities for exotic and unusual dishes.*

STEP 1

STEP 2

STEP 3

STEP 5

(BELL) PEPPERS WITH ROSEMARY BASTE

The flavour of grilled (broiled) or roasted (bell) peppers is very different from when they are eaten raw, so do try them cooked in this way. They taste even better when brushed with a crushed rosemary baste as they

SERVES 4

4 tbsp olive oil
finely grated rind of 1 lemon
4 tbsp lemon juice
1 tbsp balsamic vinegar
1 tbsp crushed fresh rosemary, or 1 tsp dried
    rosemary
2 red (bell) peppers, halved, cored and
    deseeded
2 yellow (bell) peppers, halved, cored and
    deseeded
2 tbsp pine kernels
salt and pepper
sprigs of fresh rosemary to garnish

1 Mix together the olive oil, lemon rind, lemon juice, vinegar and crushed rosemary. Season with salt and pepper.

2 Place the (bell) peppers, skin-side uppermost, on the rack of a grill (broiler) pan, lined with foil. Brush the olive oil mixture over them.

3 Cook the (bell) peppers until the skin begins to char, basting frequently with the lemon juice mixture. Remove from the heat, cover with foil to trap the steam and leave for 5 minutes.

4 Meanwhile, scatter the pine kernels on to the grill (broiler) rack and toast them lightly.

5 Peel the (bell) peppers, slice them into strips and place them in a warmed serving dish. Sprinkle with the pine kernels and drizzle any remaining lemon juice mixture over them. Garnish with sprigs of fresh rosemary and serve at once.

PEELING PEPPERS

Covering the hot (bell) peppers with a piece of foil after grilling (broiling) traps the escaping steam. This loosens their skins, so that they are easy to peel, and it helps to keep them warm.

STEP 1

STEP 2

STEP 3

STEP 4

CREAMY BAKED FENNEL

Baked fennel tastes fabulous in this creamy sauce, flavoured with caraway seeds. A crunchy breadcrumb topping gives an interesting change of texture.

SERVES 4

2 tbsp lemon juice
2 bulbs fennel, trimmed
125 g/4 oz/¹/₄ cup low-fat soft cheese
150 ml/¹/₄ pint/²/₃ cup single (light) cream
150 ml/¹/₄ pint/²/₃ cup milk
1 egg, beaten
60 g/2 oz/¹/₄ cup butter
2 tsp caraway seeds
60 g/2 oz/1 cup fresh white breadcrumbs
salt and pepper
sprigs of parsley to garnish

1 Bring a large saucepan of water to the boil and add the lemon juice. Slice the bulbs of fennel thinly and add them to the saucepan. Cook for 2–3 minutes to blanch, and then drain them well, and arrange in a buttered ovenproof baking dish.

2 Beat the soft cheese in a bowl until smooth. Add the cream, milk and beaten egg, and whisk together until combined. Season with salt and pepper and pour over the fennel.

3 Melt 15 g/¹/₂ oz of the butter in a small frying pan (skillet) and fry the caraway seeds gently for 1–2 minutes, to release their flavour and aroma. Sprinkle over the fennel.

4 Melt the remaining butter in a frying pan (skillet). Add the breadcrumbs and fry gently until lightly browned. Sprinkle evenly over the surface of the fennel.

5 Place in a preheated oven at 180°C/350°F/Gas Mark 4 and bake for 25–30 minutes, or until the fennel is tender.

6 Serve, garnished with sprigs of parsley.

ALTERNATIVE

If you cannot find any fennel in the shops, leeks make a delicious alternative. Use about 750 g/1½ lb, making sure that they are washed thoroughly to remove all traces of sand.

STEP 1

STEP 2

STEP 3

STEP 4

COURGETTE (ZUCCHINI), CARROT & FETA CHEESE PATTIES

Grated carrots, courgettes (zucchini) and Feta cheese are combined with cumin seeds, poppy seeds, curry powder and chopped parsley to make these delicious patties, which are fried gently until golden brown.

SERVES 4

2 large carrots
1 large courgette (zucchini)
1 small onion
60 g/2 oz Feta cheese
30 g/1 oz/¼ cup plain (all-purpose) flour
½ tsp cumin seeds
½ tsp poppy seeds
1 tsp medium curry powder
1 tbsp chopped fresh parsley
1 egg, beaten
30 g/1 oz/2 tbsp butter
2 tbsp vegetable oil
salt and pepper
sprigs of fresh herbs to garnish

1 Grate the carrots, courgette (zucchini), onion and Feta cheese coarsely, either by hand or in a food processor.

2 Mix together the flour, cumin seeds, poppy seeds, curry powder and parsley in a large bowl. Season well with salt and pepper.

3 Add the carrot mixture to the seasoned flour, tossing well to combine. Stir in the beaten egg and mix well.

4 Heat the butter and oil in a large frying pan (skillet). Place heaped tablespoonfuls of the carrot mixture in the pan, flattening them slightly with the back of the spoon. Fry gently for about 2 minutes on each side, until crisp and golden brown. Drain on paper towels and keep warm until all the mixture is used.

5 Serve, garnished with sprigs of fresh herbs.

VARIATION

If you want to vary the flavour of these patties, omit the cumin seeds and curry powder and substitute 1 tbsp chopped fresh oregano for the parsley.

SAUTE OF SUMMER VEGETABLES WITH TARRAGON DRESSING

The freshness of lightly cooked summer vegetables is enhanced by the aromatic flavour of the tarragon and white wine dressing, which is poured over the hot vegetables just before serving.

STEP 1

SERVES 4

250 g/8 oz baby carrots, scrubbed
125 g/4 oz runner (green) beans
2 courgettes (zucchini), trimmed
1 bunch large spring onions(scallions),
   trimmed
1 bunch radishes, trimmed
60 g/2 oz/¼ cup butter
2 tbsp light olive oil
2 tbsp white wine vinegar
4 tbsp dry white wine
1 tsp caster (superfine) sugar
1 tbsp chopped fresh tarragon
salt and pepper
sprigs of fresh tarragon to garnish

1 Trim and halve the carrots, slice the beans and courgettes (zucchini), and halve the spring onions (scallions) and radishes, so that all the vegetables are cut to even-sized pieces.

2 Melt the butter in a large frying pan (skillet) or wok. Add all the vegetables and fry them over a medium heat, stirring frequently.

3 Heat the olive oil, vinegar, white wine and sugar in a small saucepan. Remove from the heat and add the tarragon.

4 When the vegetables are just cooked, but still retain their crunchiness, pour over the 'dressing'. Stir through, and then transfer to a warmed serving dish. Garnish with sprigs of fresh tarragon and serve at once.

STEP 2

STEP 3

ALTERNATIVES

Use any combination of fresh vegetables for this dish, but remember to serve them while still slightly crunchy for the best texture and flavour. The vegetables also retain more of their nutrients when cooked this way.

If you cannot find any fresh tarragon, substitute a different herb. Marjoram, basil, oregano, chives or chervil would make delicious alternatives.

STEP 4

STEP 1

STEP 3

STEP 4

STEP 5

SPICY STUFFED CHINESE LEAVES

Mushrooms, spring onions (scallions), celery and rice are flavoured with five-spice powder and wrapped in Chinese leaves in this tasty vegetable dish. If you want to serve it as a main course, simply double the quantity.

SERVES 4

8 large Chinese leaves
60 g/2 oz/$^1/_3$ cup long-grain rice
$^1/_2$ vegetable stock (bouillon) cube
60 g/2 oz/$^1/_4$ cup butter
1 bunch spring onions (scallions), trimmed and chopped finely
1 celery stick, chopped finely
125 g/4 oz/1$^1/_4$ cups button mushrooms, sliced
1 tsp Chinese five-spice powder
300 ml/$^1/_2$ pint/1$^1/_4$ cups passatta (sieved tomato sauce)
salt and pepper
fresh chives to garnish

1 Blanch the Chinese leaves in boiling water for 1 minute. Refresh them under cold running water and drain well. Be careful not to tear them.

2 Cook the rice in plenty of boiling water, flavoured with the stock (bouillon) cube, until just tender. Drain well.

3 Meanwhile, melt the butter in a frying pan (skillet) and fry the spring onions (scallions) and celery gently for 3–4 minutes until softened, but not browned. Add the mushrooms and

cook for a further 3–4 minutes, stirring frequently.

4 Add the cooked rice to the pan with the five-spice powder. Season with salt and pepper and stir well to combine the ingredients.

5 Lay out the Chinese leaves on a work surface (counter) and divide the rice mixture between them. Roll each leaf into a neat parcel to enclose the stuffing. Place them, seam-side down, in a greased ovenproof dish. Pour the passatta over them and cover with foil.

6 Bake in a preheated oven at 190°C/375°F/Gas Mark 5 for 25–30 minutes. Serve immediately, garnished with chives.

CABBAGE LEAVES

Cabbage leaves, either from a hard white variety or from a more leafy spring cabbage, can be used instead of Chinese leaves. Take care when removing the leaves and blanching them, to prevent them from tearing.

STEP 1

STEP 2

STEP 3

STEP 4

STIR-FRIED WINTER VEGETABLES WITH CORIANDER (CILANTRO)

Ordinary winter vegetables are given extraordinary treatment in this lively stir-fry, just the thing for perking up jaded palates.

SERVES 4

3 tbsp sesame oil
30 g/1 oz/¼ cup blanched almonds
1 large carrot, cut into thin strips
1 large turnip, cut into thin strips
1 onion, sliced finely
1 garlic clove, crushed
3 celery sticks, sliced finely
125 g/4 oz Brussels sprouts, trimmed and
    halved
125 g/4 oz cauliflower, broken into florets
125 g/4 oz/2 cups white cabbage, shredded
2 tsp sesame seeds
1 tsp grated fresh root ginger
½ tsp medium chilli powder
1 tbsp chopped fresh coriander (cilantro)
1 tbsp light soy sauce
salt and pepper
sprigs of fresh coriander (cilantro) to
    garnish

1 Heat the sesame oil in a wok or large frying pan (skillet). Stir-fry the almonds until lightly browned, then lift them out and drain on paper towels.

2 Add all the vegetables to the wok or frying pan (skillet), except for the cabbage. Stir-fry briskly for 3–4 minutes.

3 Add the cabbage, sesame seeds, ginger and chilli powder to the vegetables and cook, stirring, for 2 minutes.

4 Add the chopped coriander (cilantro), soy sauce and almonds to the mixture, stirring them through gently. Serve the vegetables, garnished with sprigs of fresh coriander (cilantro).

SESAME OIL

Substitute different winter vegetables, to make a change. Try leeks, parsnips, swede (rutabaga), salsify, celeriac or red cabbage as alternatives.

Sesame oil is not essential for making this stir-fry, but it does give an excellent flavour and is a typical ingredient of oriental cookery, though it is generally used for sprinkling over food or flavouring sauces. Vegetable or olive oil could be used instead, or groundnut or corn oil, which are frequently used in Chinese cooking.

CHAPTER FIVE

Salads

With the range of fresh produce that is now widely available, dull or lifeless salads should be a thing of the past. In this selection you will discover a number of bright ideas bursting with flavour and colour. Make one of these salads to accompany your main meal, or make larger portions to serve alone. You could also select a recipe from this chapter to serve as a starter.

Some of these recipes are light and fruity, others are more substantial. Choose the right salad to serve with your main course choice to offer a good balance – make sure that the flavours and textures complement rather than clash with one another. Alternatively, make a selection of these salads to serve at parties and buffets with lots of crusty new bread, a tempting cheese board and plenty of fresh fruit for an irresistible spread.

The secret of a successful salad relies on two important aspects: the freshness of the ingredients and the choice of a complementary dressing to bring out their flavours. Choose your salad ingredients carefully, buying them at the peak of perfection. They will then taste superb, especially when combined with one of the unusual dressings suggested. So try some of the ideas in this chapter and discover some sensational new salads to add to your repertoire.

Opposite: *Both fruits and vegetables can be used to make delicious and refreshing salads, which will add colour, texture and flavour to any meal.*

STEP 1

STEP 2

STEP 3

STEP 4

MARINATED VEGETABLE SALAD

Lightly steamed vegetables taste superb served slightly warm in a marinade of olive oil, white wine, vinegar and fresh herbs.

SERVES 4–6

175 g/6 oz baby carrots, trimmed
2 celery hearts, cut into 4 pieces
125g/4 oz sugar snap peas or mangetout
  (snow peas)
1 bulb fennel, sliced
175 g/6 oz small asparagus spears
15 g/¹/₂ oz/1¹/₂ tbsp sunflower seeds
sprigs of fresh dill to garnish

DRESSING:
4 tbsp olive oil
4 tbsp dry white wine
2 tbsp white wine vinegar
1 tbsp chopped fresh dill
1 tbsp chopped parsley
salt and pepper

1 Steam the carrots, celery, sugar snap peas or mangetout (snow peas), fennel and asparagus over gently boiling water until just tender. It is important that they retain a little 'bite'.

2 Meanwhile, mix together the olive oil, wine, vinegar and chopped herbs. Season well with salt and pepper.

3 When the vegetables are cooked, transfer them to a serving dish and pour over the dressing at once. The hot vegetables will absorb the flavour of the dressing as they cool.

4 Scatter the sunflower seeds on a baking sheet and toast them under a preheated grill (broiler) until lightly browned. Sprinkle them over the vegetables.

5 Serve the salad while the vegetables are still slightly warm, garnished with sprigs of fresh dill.

VARIATION

Sesame seeds or pine kernels can be used instead of sunflower seeds for sprinkling over the vegetables. Keep an eye on them while grilling, as they can burn easily.

STEP 1

STEP 2

STEP 4

STEP 4

RED ONION, CHERRY TOMATO & PASTA SALAD

Pasta tastes perfect in this lively salad, dressed with red wine vinegar, lemon juice, basil and olive oil. Sliced red onions, roast (bell) peppers, courgettes (zucchini) and tomatoes add wonderful flavours and colours.

SERVES 4

175 g/6 oz/1½ cups pasta shapes
1 yellow (bell) pepper, halved, cored and
    deseeded
2 small courgettes (zucchini), sliced
1 red onion, sliced thinly
125 g/4 oz cherry tomatoes, halved
a handful of fresh basil leaves, torn into
    small pieces
salt and pepper
sprigs of fresh basil to garnish

DRESSING:
60 ml/4 tbsp olive oil
30 ml/2 tbsp red wine vinegar
2 tsp lemon juice
1 tsp Dijon mustard
½ tsp caster (superfine) sugar

1 Cook the pasta in plenty of boiling, lightly salted water for about 8 minutes, or until just tender.

2 Meanwhile, place the (bell) pepper halves, skin-side uppermost, under a preheated grill (broiler) until they just begin to char. Leave them to cool, then peel and slice them into strips.

3 Cook the courgettes (zucchini) in a small amount of boiling, lightly salted water for 3–4 minutes, until cooked, yet still crunchy. Drain and refresh under cold running water to cool quickly.

4 To make the dressing, mix together the olive oil, red wine vinegar, lemon juice, mustard and sugar. Season well with salt and pepper. Add the basil leaves.

5 Drain the pasta well and tip it into a large serving bowl. Add the dressing and toss well. Add the pepper, courgettes (zucchini), onion and cherry tomatoes, stirring to combine. Cover and leave at room temperature for about 30 minutes to allow the flavours to develop.

6 Serve, garnished with sprigs of fresh basil.

PASTA SHAPES

Choose pasta shapes that hold the dressing well for this salad. Conchiglie (pasta shells) or torchietti (little torches) are ideal. Properly cooked pasta retains a little 'bite', which is especially important when eaten in salads.

STEP 1

STEP 2

STEP 3

STEP 5

MELON, MANGO & GRAPE SALAD WITH GINGER & HONEY DRESSING

A little freshly grated root ginger mixed with creamy yogurt and clear honey makes a perfect dressing for this refreshing melon salad.

SERVES 4

1 cantaloup melon
60 g/2 oz/¹/₂ cup black grapes, halved and pipped
60 g/2 oz/¹/₂ cup green grapes
1 large mango
1 bunch of watercress, trimmed
iceberg lettuce leaves, shredded
2 tbsp olive oil
1 tbsp cider vinegar
1 passion fruit
salt and pepper

DRESSING:
150 ml/¹/₄ pint/²/₃ cup natural thick, full-fat yogurt
1 tbsp clear honey
1 tsp grated fresh root ginger

1 To make the dressing for the melon, mix together the yogurt, honey and ginger.

2 Halve the melon and scoop out the seeds. Slice, peel and cut into chunks. Mix with the grapes.

3 Slice the mango on each side of its large flat stone (pit). On each mango half, slash the flesh into a criss-cross pattern down to, but not through,

the skin. Push the skin from underneath to turn the mango halves inside out. Now remove the flesh and add to the melon mixture.

4 Arrange the watercress and lettuce on 4 serving plates. Make the dressing for the salad leaves (greens) by mixing together the olive oil and cider vinegar with a little salt and pepper. Drizzle over the watercress and lettuce.

5 Divide the melon mixture between the 4 plates and spoon over the yogurt dressing. Scoop the seeds out of the passion fruit and sprinkle them over the salads.

GINGER

Grated fresh root ginger gives a great flavour to this recipe, but if you can't get it, substitute ¹/₂ teaspoon of ground ginger instead.

THREE-BEAN SALAD

Fresh dwarf (thin) green beans are combined with canned soya beans and red kidney beans in a chive and tomato dressing, to make a quick and tasty salad.

STEP 1

SERVES 4–6

3 tbsp olive oil
1 tbsp lemon juice
1 tbsp tomato purée (paste)
1 tbsp light malt vinegar
1 tbsp chopped fresh chives
175 g/6 oz dwarf (thin) green beans
425 g/14 oz can soya beans, rinsed and
    drained
425 g/14 oz can red kidney beans, rinsed
    and drained
2 tomatoes, chopped
4 spring onions (scallions), trimmed and
    chopped
125 g/4 oz Feta cheese, cut into cubes
salt and pepper
mixed salad leaves (greens) to serve
chopped fresh chives to garnish

1 Put the olive oil, lemon juice, tomato purée, vinegar and chives into a large bowl and whisk together until thoroughly combined.

2 Cook the dwarf (thin) green beans in a little boiling, lightly salted water until just cooked, about 4–5 minutes. Drain, refresh under cold running water and drain well.

STEP 2

3 Add the green beans, soya beans and red kidney beans to the dressing, stirring to mix together.

4 Add the tomatoes, spring onions and Feta cheese to the bean mixture, tossing gently to coat in the dressing. Season well with salt and pepper.

5 Arrange the mixed salad leaves on 4 serving plates. Pile the bean salad on to the plates and garnish with chopped chives.

STEP 3

BEANS

You can substitute different types of canned beans for the soya beans and red kidney beans. Try haricot (navy) beans, black-eye beans (peas) or chick-peas (garbanzo beans) instead.

STEP 4

STEP 1

STEP 2

STEP 3

STEP 4

MOROCCAN ORANGE & COUS-COUS SALAD

Cous-cous is wonderful in salads as it readily takes up the flavour of the dressing. It is a semolina-based food made from durum wheat, and it simply has to be soaked to swell the grains before use.

SERVES 4–6

175 g/6 oz/2 cups cous-cous
1 bunch spring onions (scallions), trimmed
  and chopped finely
1 small green (bell) pepper, deseeded and
  chopped
10 cm/4 inch piece of cucumber, chopped
175 g/6 oz can chick-peas (garbanzo
  beans), rinsed and drained
60 g/2 oz/⅓ cup sultanas (golden raisins)
  or raisins
2 oranges
salt and pepper
lettuce leaves to serve
sprigs of fresh mint to garnish

DRESSING:
finely grated rind of 1 orange
1 tbsp chopped fresh mint
150 ml/¼ pint/⅔ cup natural yogurt

1 Put the cous-cous into a bowl and cover with boiling water. Leave it to soak for about 15 minutes to swell the grains, then stir with a fork to separate them.

2 Add the spring onions (scallions), green (bell) pepper, cucumber, chick-peas (garbanzo beans) and sultanas (golden raisins) or raisins to the cous-cous, stirring to combine. Season well with salt and pepper.

3 To make the dressing, mix together the orange rind, mint and yogurt. Pour over the cous-cous mixture and stir well.

4 Using a sharp serrated knife, remove the peel and pith from the oranges. Cut them into segments, removing all the membrane.

5 Arrange the lettuce leaves on 4 serving plates. Divide the cous-cous mixture between the plates and arrange the orange segments on top. Garnish with sprigs of fresh mint and serve.

ORANGE JUICE

When preparing the oranges, catch any juice in a bowl so that it can be stirred through the salad.

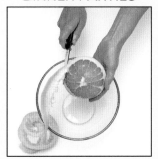

STEP 2

STEP 3

STEP 4

STEP 5

PINK GRAPEFRUIT, AVOCADO & DOLCELATTE SALAD

Fresh pink grapefruit segments, ripe avocados and sliced Italian Dolcelatte cheese make a deliciously different salad combination.

SERVES 4

¹/₂ cos (romaine) lettuce
¹/₂ oak leaf lettuce
2 pink grapefruit
2 ripe avocados
175 g/6 oz Dolcelatte cheese, sliced thinly
sprigs of fresh basil to garnish

DRESSING:
4 tbsp olive oil
1 tbsp white wine vinegar
salt and pepper

1 Arrange the lettuce leaves on 4 serving plates or in a salad bowl.

2 Remove the peel and pith from the grapefruit with a sharp serrated knife, catching the grapefruit juice in a bowl.

3 Segment the grapefruit by cutting down each side of the membrane. Remove all the membrane. Arrange the segments on the serving plates.

4 Peel, stone (pit) and slice the avocados, dipping them in the grapefruit juice to prevent them from going brown. Arrange the slices on the salad with the Dolcelatte cheese.

5 To make the dressing, combine any remaining grapefruit juice with the olive oil and wine vinegar. Season with salt and pepper, mixing well.

6 Drizzle the dressing over the salads. Garnish with fresh basil leaves and serve at once.

TIPS

Pink grapefruit segments make a very attractive colour combination with the avocados, but ordinary grapefruit will work just as well.
 To help avocados to ripen, keep them at room temperature in a brown paper bag.

VEGETARIAN COOKING

NUTRITION

Like any well-balanced diet, variety is the key, so make sure that you eat many different types of food to ensure that all the body's needs are met.

Vegetarians eating a wide variety of foods should have no problem in obtaining enough B vitamins from their food, although vegans (who do not eat dairy products) need to include a B12 supplement in their diet, or they must make sure that some of the foods they eat are specially fortified with vitamin B12.

As vitamin C can be lost during cooking, you must take care when boiling vegetables to prevent its loss. Use a small amount of water to prevent the vitamin from leaching out and being thrown away – remember this next time you cook cabbage or spinach!

Eat foods that are rich in vitamin C with iron-rich foods, as it helps to increase the uptake of iron; and avoid drinking tea, coffee and certain soft drinks with foods that contain vitamin C, as the caffeine in them can decrease how much vitamin C your body subsequently absorbs.

Vitamin D is often known as the 'sunshine vitamin', as the body can manufacture its own supply from exposure to sunlight.

VEGETARIAN NUTRITION

People choose to eat vegetarian food for all sorts of different reasons, whether it is on moral grounds, for health reasons, for economy or simply because they prefer the flavour of vegetarian food. These days, far more people are choosing to eat vegetarian food at least some of the time, to make an interesting change or to reduce their food bill. Whatever the motive, one thing is certain – everyone enjoys good food, and vegetarian food can be as good as, and often better than, traditional meat and fish dishes. So dispel the myth that vegetarian cooking can be complicated, time-consuming, heavy or stodgy. Choose recipes that are fun to cook as well as to eat, and which are full of vibrant colours and exciting flavours. Experiment with exotic fruit, vegetables, herbs and spices as well as the vast range of grains and pulses that are staple foods in other countries. Vegetarian meals are perfect for entertaining or just for the family to enjoy, and can easily be adapted to suit all tastes.

Getting the balance right

Vegetarian food is extremely healthy, and provides all the important vitamins, minerals, proteins, carbohydrates and fats that make up a nutritious, balanced diet. And because you tend to eat more fruit, vegetables, grains and pulses, the diet is rich in complex carbohydrates, your primary source of energy, as well in fibre, which helps to keep the body healthy from the inside.

There is no problem in obtaining sufficient protein in a well-balanced vegetarian diet – there are lots of foods to choose from. Eggs, cheese, milk, nuts and beans, soya products such as TVP (texturized vegetable protein), soya milk and tofu, Quorn or mycoprotein are all good sources. Be sure to eat a wide range of these foods, so that your body gets the full range of proteins that it needs.

One additional benefit of following a vegetarian diet is that it can be quite low in fat. The main sources of fat in your diet will be from vegetable, nut and olive oils, butter and margarine, nuts and any products containing these ingredients. So slimmers can succeed in losing weight by following a vegetarian diet, providing they keep an eye on their overall fat intake. Complex carbohydrates such as brown rice, oats and wholemeal (whole wheat) pasta are particularly useful to dieters, as they ensure a steady release of energy and a stable blood sugar level, preventing the fatigue and hunger often associated with dieting.

For supplies of vitamins in a vegetarian diet, you shouldn't go far wrong. Fruit and vegetables are packed with important vitamins, essential for our general well-being and the healthy functioning of our bodies.

For vitamin A, the best sources are yellow fruits and vegetables and some green vegetables – apricots, peaches, spinach and carrots, for example. It is also present in butter and added to margarines. Vitamin A helps us to resist infections and keeps our skin, hair, eyes and body tissues healthy.

The B group vitamins help us to release the energy that we take in as food, acting as a kind of catalyst. They are also needed to maintain a healthy nervous system and healthy red blood cells. Apart from vitamin B12, all the B vitamins can be found in yeast and wholegrain cereals, especially wheat flour and wheatgerm.

Vitamin C is well known for helping to prevent infections and is believed by many to help ward off winter colds and 'flu. It also plays an important role in assisting the absorption of iron. Fresh fruit, leafy vegetables, tomatoes, (bell) peppers and potatoes are all good sources, so include plenty in your diet.

The other important vitamin is D, which is essential for maintaining strong bones and teeth, by enabling the body to absorb calcium. Good food sources include eggs, cheese, margarine and butter.

Minerals are the other vital nutrient essential for our good health and well-being. These are the elements that are needed by the body in tiny amounts, but they are needed regularly, so it is wise to know about them and ensure that you include enough foods containing them in your diet. Calcium is found in milk, cheese, yogurt and other dairy products, leafy green vegetables, bread, nuts, seeds and dried fruits. Iron is found in beans, seeds, nuts, eggs, cocoa and chocolate, wholemeal bread, leafy green vegetables and dried fruits (especially apricots and figs). Other minerals important in the diet include magnesium, phosphorus, potassium and zinc, but there should be

no problem in obtaining sufficient quantities of these elements if you eat a wide variety of foods.

THE VEGETARIAN SHOPPING BASKET

When shopping for vegetarian foods, be sure that you are not buying animal products unawares – you may have to make one or two changes here and there. Choose cheese that is made from vegetarian rennet; buy agar-agar or gelozone instead of gelatine; select a vegetarian suet instead of beef suet – no, you won't have to forego delicious dumplings or suet puddings!

Be aware of what you are spreading on your bread too. Some margarines are not suitable as they contain both fish oils and animal fats, so check that you are buying one made entirely of vegetable oil. Butter is perfect, unless you are a vegan and choose to eat only those foods that are from plant sources.

THE VEGETARIAN STORE CUPBOARD

A well-stocked store-cupboard forms the backbone of any good cook's kitchen, and it is always useful to have plenty of basic foods ready to hand. Use the following information as a checklist for when you need to replenish your stocks.

Flours, grains, pasta and pulses

You will need to keep a selection of flours – plain (all-purpose) and self-raising (self-rising), strong flour if you want to make your own bread and yeast bakes, and buy wholemeal (whole wheat) flour too, for using on its own or for combining with white flour for cakes and pastries. You may also like to keep some rice flour and

Ingredients

To give variety and interest to your cooking, experiment with different seasonings, spices and herbs, and try out some of the wonderful array of oils and vinegars that are now so widely available.

When choosing your rice, remember that brown rice – or unpolished rice – is a better source of vitamin B1 and fibre.

It is important to cook dried red and black kidney beans in plenty of vigorously boiling water for 15 minutes to destroy harmful toxins in the outer skin. Drain and rinse the beans, and then continue to simmer until the beans are tender. Soya beans should be boiled for 1 hour, as they contain a substance that inhibits protein from being absorbed.

If you are short of time, canned beans will do just as well. If you prefer, choose brands that contain no added sugar or salt, and rinse them well before using. Once opened, they will keep in the fridge for several days, but don't leave them in the tin – transfer them to a bowl, and cover them up.

Try grinding your own spices with a mortar and pestle, or in a coffee mill, to make your own blends, or just experiment with those that you can buy. Although spices will keep well, don't leave them in the cupboard for too long, as they may lose some of their strength. It's a good idea to label each packet with the date on which you bought it, as this will help you to keep track.

To bring out the flavour of nuts and seeds, grill or roast them until lightly browned.

When buying dried fruits, look for those that have not been treated with anything: buy figs that have not been rolled in sugar, for example, and choose unsulphured apricots, if they are available. Also, check the fruit over for bits of dried stalk and grit, which can creep in very occasionally.

Oils and fats
Olive oil tastes wonderful as a basis for salad dressings. A fine fruity virgin oil from the first pressing makes a deliciously robust dressing, or choose a lighter oil to give a dressing with a more delicate flavour. It is a good tip to dress hot pasta with a couple of tablespoons of good quality home-made salad dressing. The flavour is absorbed, and it helps to prevent the pasta from sticking.

A good way of making the most of day-old French bread or Italian ciabatta is to slice it, place it on a baking tray and drizzle it with olive oil. Top with sliced tomatoes, grated cheese and slivers of black olives, and then bake in a hot oven for a few minutes.

cornflour (cornstarch) (from maize) for thickening sauces and to add to cakes, biscuits and puddings. Buckwheat, chick-pea (garbanzo bean) and soya flours can also be bought – useful for pancakes and for combining with other flours to add different flavours and textures.

Keep a good variety of grains – for rice choose from long-grain, basmati, Italian arborio for making risotto, short-grain for puddings, wild rice to add interest. Look out for fragrant Thai rice, jasmine rice and combinations of different varieties to add colour and texture to your dishes.

Other grains add variety to the diet – try to include some barley (whole grain or pearl), millet, bulgur wheat, polenta (made from maize) oats (oatmeal, oatflakes or oatbran), semolina – including cous-cous (from which it is made), sago and tapioca.

Pasta has become much more popular recently, and there are many types and shapes to choose from. Keep a good selection, and always make sure you have the basic lasagne sheets, tagliatelle or fettucine (noodles) and spaghetti. Try spinach or tomato varieties for a change and sample some of the fresh pastas that you can now buy.

Pulses, such as soya beans, haricot (navy) beans, red kidney and cannellini beans, chick-peas (garbanzo beans), all types of lentils, split peas and butter beans are very important in a vegetarian diet as they are a good protein source, and contain vitamins and minerals. Buy them dried for soaking and cooking yourself, or buy canned varieties for speed and convenience.

Spices and herbs
A good selection of spices and herbs is important for adding variety and interest to your cooking – add to your range each time you try a new recipe. There are some good spice mixtures available – try Cajun seasoning, Chinese five-spice powder, Indonesian piri-piri seasoning and various curry blends available.

Fresh herbs are always preferable to dried, but it is essential to have dried ones in stock as a useful back-up to use when fresh are unavailable. Keep the basics such as thyme, rosemary, bay leaves and some good Mediterranean mixtures for Italian and French cooking.

Nuts and seeds
As well as adding protein, vitamins and useful fats to the diet, nuts and seeds add important flavour and texture to vegetarian meals. Make sure that you keep a good supply of almonds, brazils, cashews, chestnuts (in cans), hazelnuts, peanuts, pecans, pistachios, pine kernels (nuts) and walnuts. Coconut – either creamed or desiccated (shredded) – is useful too.

For your seed collection, have sesame, sunflower, pumpkin and poppy. Pumpkin seeds, in particular, are an excellent source of zinc.

Dried fruits
Currants, raisins, sultanas (golden raisins), dates, apples, apricots, figs, pears, peaches, prunes, paw-paws, mangoes, figs, bananas and pineapples can all be purchased dried and can be used in lots of different recipes. Though they are a healthier alternative to

biscuits (cookies) and sweets (candies), dried fruits are still high in calories, so although they are a natural source of sugar, eat them in moderation as a treat.

Oils and fats

Useful for adding subtle flavourings to foods, it is a good idea to have a selection in store. Have a light olive oil for cooking and an extra-virgin one for salad dressings. Use sunflower oil as a good general purpose oil and select one or two speciality oils to add character to different dishes. Sesame oil is wonderful in stir-fries; hazelnut and walnut oils are superb in salad dressings.

Oils and fats add flavour to foods, and contain the important fat-soluble vitamins A, D, E and K. It is a good idea to keep an eye on how much you use, especially if you are watcing your weight, as all fats and oils are high in calories. It is worth pointing out that oils are simply fats that are liquid at room temperature, and they are higher in calories than butter or margarine. (Oils contain 100% fat; butter and margarine contain 80% fat.)

Vinegars

Choose three or four vinegars – red or white wine, cider, light malt, tarragon, sherry or balsamic vinegar, to name just a few – each will add its own character to your recipes.

Useful extras

Hot chilli sauce, soy sauce, tahini (sesame seed paste), yeast extract, sea salt, black and green peppercorns, tomato and garlic purées (pastes),

vegetable stock (bouillon) cubes, dried yeast, gelozone or agar-agar are all useful store-cupboard additions.

THE VEGETARIAN FRIDGE AND FREEZER

Thankfully, food manufacturers have wised up to the fact that lots of us love to eat vegetarian food, so it is now possible to choose from a huge range of prepared meals from the chilled or frozen food cabinets. These are excellent standbys for meals in a hurry and they add variety and choice to the diet. It is useful to stock up on a few favourites for those times when you need to prepare food fast. Pasta dishes, vegetable bakes and burgers, curries, flans and quiches are just some of the dishes to choose from.

The secret of success

As with any cooking, the choice of ingredients is of paramount importance. If they are fresh and of high quality, you are well on your way to achieving delicious food. Not only will the flavours be better, but so will the colours, textures and nutritive value. Fresh fruit and vegetables lose their vitamin content very quickly if stored too long, so buy from the freshest possible source, and use soon after buying.

It is also important to follow the recipe procedure correctly, so this book's step-by-step format is ideal. Its photographs and instructions will guide you through each recipe, showing you clearly and concisely exactly what is needed – and when. It is also important to experiment – so use these recipes as a stepping stone to your own delicious inventions.

When you are making dressings or adding oil to a wok or frying pan, it is a good idea to measure it – one tablespoon of oil contains 120 calories. (One level tablespoonful of butter or margarine contains 105 calories.) It is easy to use twice as much without realising, doubling your fat intake without making any difference to the taste.

If you are trying to lose weight, reduce your fat intake where possible, not only by cutting down on the 'visible' fats like oils, margarine and butter, but by trying to reduce the foods containing hidden fats, such as hard cheese, nuts, pastries, cakes and biscuits. And watch those calorie-laden salad dressings and mayonnaise too! Cut out all fried foods while dieting and reduce the number of foods that are high in sugar, and try to resist sweets and chocolate bars.

Taking stock

Besides stocking a selection of ready-made meals, freeze other basics such as frozen pastries (shortcrust, filo or puff pastry); a selection of breads, such as pitta, French bread, rolls or part-baked bread; pre-cooked pasta dishes, pasta sauces, stocks, breadcrumbs, home-made soups and sauces, flan cases, pancakes, pizza bases, and so on. All these will be useful when you are short of time.

INDEX